EXPERIENCING
THE SPIRIT

Living in the active
presence of God

YOUTH WITH A MISSION

ZondervanPublishingHouse
Grand Rapids, Michigan

A Division of HarperCollinsPublishers

GET CONNECTED!
Living Encounters Series

Experiencing the Spirit
Copyright © 2000 Youth With A Mission

Requests for information should be addressed to:

🏭 ZondervanPublishingHouse
Grand Rapids, Michigan 49530

ISBN 0-310-22706-2

All Scripture quotations, unless otherwise indicated, are taken from the *Holy Bible: New International Version*®. NIV®. Copyright © 1973, 1978, 1984 by International Bible Society. Used by permission of Zondervan Publishing House. All rights reserved.

The articles on pages 15, 27, 29, 36, 38, 42, 46, 65, 70–71, 90–97 are excerpted from Youth With A Mission study notes in *The Christian Growth Study Bible*, © 1997 by The Zondervan Corporation. Study notes © 1997 by Youth With A Mission.

The Living Encounters Bible study series was produced through a dynamic team process of Youth With A Mission staff members, although each guide was created by one primary author. The team consisted of: Betty Barnett, Retha Badenhorst, Maureen Menard, Ruth Perrin, Ed Sherman, Donna Jo Taylor, and Christine Terrasson. The primary author of Experiencing the Spirit *was Maureen Menard.*

Interior design by Sherri Hoffman

Printed in the United States of America

00 01 02 03 04 05 /❖ EP/ 10 9 8 7 6 5 4 3 2

Contents

foreword
Close Encounters with the Living God

Welcome to the Living Encounters Bible study series! We created this unique study to help sincere seekers find a deeper revelation of God. Our God loves to be pursued. He wants us to know and love him more, and there's no better way to learn of his character and his ways than through his written Word.

The Living Encounters series offers exciting new ways for you to engage Scripture and apply its truth to your life. Through this series, each participant is encouraged into living encounters with God, his Spirit, his Word, his people, and his world.

Some elements of the study are drawn from teaching methods that have been used for decades in our Discipleship Training Schools. As our students encounter God, their perspective on life changes radically. The very truth of the Scripture connects them to the global picture, to God's heart for the peoples of the world. Therefore, the more they come to know God, the more they want to make him known.

The Living Encounters series is a wonderful Bible study tool for people of various levels of spiritual maturity. Its flexible, user-friendly format appeals to people with different learning styles and cultural perspectives. And when coupled with the teaching aids found in the Christian Growth Study Bible (Zondervan), the series is a highly effective way to draw new understanding and guidance from the Scriptures.

May this series bring you a whole new appreciation of our awesome God—and set you on the pathway to many living encounters!

—Loren Cunningham,
Founder of Youth With A Mission

Introducing Living Encounters

Did you ever hear about a person you'd never met—what he said, what he looked like, what he did—and then you met him, and somehow the picture you had formed in your mind didn't fit at all? For better or worse, you were confronted with reality! An "encounter" does not mean a secondhand report about a person or a situation; it means a face-to-face meeting. In an encounter, you meet a person, and your knowledge about him or her combines with and adapts to the living reality.

This is what "Living Encounters" is all about. You have read God's Word, the Bible, but there is a gap between what it says and what you experience. You know God's Spirit is alive and well, but life would be a lot simpler if he sat down beside you and gave you advice. You like people, but sometimes loving them seems impossible. And then there's the whole world out there—so full of need and suffering that you don't know how to even begin to help.

Living Encounters are more than an analysis of Bible passages or a tool for group discussion. They are to help you *meet* and adjust your life to God's Word, God's Spirit, God's people, and God's world. They are designed to challenge you not only to grasp truth but to live it out, to connect it to your personal world and to the larger world around you. As you apply yourself to these studies, you can expect exciting changes both in your thinking and in your lifestyle.

The Living Encounters series is versatile. Each guide is divided into six sessions and can be used within a small-group discussion in a church or on a college campus. However, the series is designed so that it is just as effective for individual study.

The guides are personal. They constantly lead you to ask, "What does this mean to me and how do I apply it in my own life?" Questions reveal needs and desires of the heart and invite you to embrace the promises, assurances, exhortations, and challenges of God's Word. As you respond, the Spirit of God will be responding to you, renewing your mind and transforming you more into the likeness of Jesus Christ — the ultimate goal of all Bible study.

The Features

Each session includes the following basic features.

Opening Vignette

To draw you into the topic at hand, each session opens with a thought-provoking narrative.

Preparing Heart and Mind

These questions open your heart and focus your mind on what God wants to say to you in the passage. If you are using Living Encounters in a group setting, we strongly encourage you to include this section during the first fifteen minutes of your discussion. Please realize, however, that the entire study will probably take about an hour and fifteen minutes. If you don't have that much time, then ask your group members to reflect on these questions before you meet together, and begin your discussion with the section "Engaging the Text."

Setting the Stage

The background information found in this sidebar will help you better understand the context of the study.

Engaging the Text

This important section leads you through a Bible passage using inductive Bible study questions. The inductive method prompts you to observe, interpret, and apply the Bible passage with a variety of question styles:

- Observation questions will help you focus on what the Bible says.
- Interpretation questions will help you step into the world of the original readers to understand better what the passage meant to them.
- Application questions will help you to apply the truth to your heart and present circumstances.

Responding to God

In this section, you will receive suggestions that will help you focus your individual or group prayer time.

Punch Line

This brief sentence or verse will reinforce the theme of the session.

Taking It Further

This section is designed to be completed between studies to reinforce and further apply what you have learned. It offers a variety of suggestions for connecting what you have studied to your everyday life.

- **Connecting to Life:** a variety of activities to stimulate your personal growth and ministry to others.
- **Digging Deeper:** additional Scriptures give a deeper and broader understanding of what the Bible says about the topic of the study.
- **Meditation:** a time to reflect more deeply on a specific verse or passage.
- **Personal Expression:** creative suggestions help you to process and apply what you've learned in the session.
- **World Focus:** an encouragement to look beyond your personal realm to the needs of our world.

Additional Features

In addition to the above, the guides contain a variety of optional features. All are designed to appeal to different learning styles and gifts and to encourage deeper integration of material into all of life. It is expected that you will choose whatever features you find most useful for each session. These optional features, found in articles throughout the sessions, include:

- Gray boxed material: often these will be devotional articles relevant to the study.
- People of Impact: a snapshot of the life of a person who models the principles studied.
- People Profile: a brief description of a people group that needs to be reached with the gospel.
- Hot Topic: a discussion starter to use with other group members to stimulate deeper thinking on a difficult subject.

Leader's Notes

Leader's notes for each session are provided at the back of each study guide.

Suggestions for Individual or Group Study

Preparing Heart and Mind

1. Ask the Lord for insight, wisdom, and grace to understand the Bible passage and apply it to your own life.
2. Choose one or more of the preparation questions and take time to think about it.

Engaging the Text

1. Read and reread the assigned Bible passage. You may find it helpful to have several different translations. A good literal translation rather than a paraphrase is recommended, such as the *New International Version*, the *New American Standard Bible*, the *New Revised Standard Version*, and the *New King James Bible*. The questions in each study are based on the *New International Version*. A Bible dictionary can also serve you well for look-

ing up any unfamiliar words, people, places, or theological concepts. Commentaries, while having great value, are not part of this kind of study, which uses the inductive method.

2. The questions are designed to help you make observations, draw conclusions, and apply God's truth to your life. Write your answers in the space provided. Recording your observations and conclusions is an important step in any study process. It encourages you to think through your answers thoroughly, thus furthering the learning process.

3. Note the optional elements offered in the sidebars. These are designed to encourage greater understanding of the passage being studied.

4. Be aware of the continuous presence of the Lord throughout the process. You may want to stop and pray in the midst of your study. Be sure to end your study with a time of waiting, listening, and responding to the Lord in prayer.

5. Be willing to participate in the discussion. The leader of the group will not be lecturing; rather, he or she will be encouraging the members of the group to discuss what they have learned from the passage. The leader will be asking the questions that are found in this guide. Plan to share what God has taught you in your individual study time.

6. Stick to the passage being studied. Your answers should be based on the verses which are the focus of the discussion and not on outside authorities such as commentators or speakers (or the commentary notes in your study Bible!).

7. Be sensitive to other members of the group. Listen attentively when they share. You can learn a lot from their insights! Stick with the topic — when you have insights on a different subject, keep it for another time so the group is not distracted from the focus of the study.

8. Be careful not to dominate the discussion. We are sometimes so eager to share that we leave too little opportunity for others to contribute. By all means participate, but allow others to do so as well.

9. Expect the Holy Spirit to teach you both through the passage and through other members of the group. Everyone has a unique perspective that can broaden your own understanding. Pray that you will have an enjoyable and profitable time together.
10. The "Responding to God" section is the place where you pray about the topics you have studied. At this time you will invite the Holy Spirit to work these truths further into each of your lives. Be careful not to overlook this essential aspect of your time together.

Taking It Further

1. Identify other questions that arise through the study so that you can pursue them later.
2. Choose one or more of the activities to help you apply the principles in your life. These are optional activities to be done on your own after the Bible study session.

Leader's Notes

If you are the discussion leader or simply want further information, you will find additional suggestions and ideas for each session in the Leader's Notes in the back of this guide.

Experiencing the Spirit: Living in the Active Presence of God

Mike couldn't bear to listen to one more word of the sermon. He was fed up with being challenged to "be like Jesus," without any instructions on how to do it! "How am I supposed to know what Jesus would do if he were in my shoes?" he fumed to himself. "Of course I know there are things he would have said no to, but that was Jesus! Where am I supposed to get the power that he had to say no to those things?" Mike's mind wandered to what it would have been like to be one of Jesus' disciples. Imagine actually being there, watching, learning, seeing how he handled life! He longed for Jesus to be with him now, in flesh and blood.

What Mike really needed was a reminder of Jesus' own words to his original disciples, as recorded in John's gospel. As wonderful as it was for Peter, John, and the other disciples to have Jesus with them in physical form, Jesus knew that they—and us—would be much better off when he was gone. Why? Jesus returned to the Father, having canceled our debt of sin through the cross, so that the Holy Spirit could live within those who believe in him.

In his last week before going to the cross, Jesus spoke often to his disciples about the Holy Spirit, who would soon "indwell" them. He promised that the Spirit would give them comfort, understanding, and instruction, and he would provide an inner link to God the Father.

This study looks at the Holy Spirit's personal and powerful ministry within the life of the believer. If you are looking for a greater awareness that God is with you, freedom from lies that seem to cripple you, and a deeper sense of true satisfaction . . .

. . . then this study is for you!

Assures Us of His Presence
John 14:15–27; 16:5–15

session
ONE

"I don't know how to tell you this, Joe," Alan blurted out to his colleague, "but I'm facing a powerful sexual temptation with one of my students. It's not to the point of any real physical involvement yet, but my mind often drifts to imagining it. I just don't know how to stop what's happening." Alan fell silent, tense, and anxious.

Joe sat quietly, listening for wisdom from the Holy Spirit. After a moment, he asked, "Alan, when you're imagining the sin, where is Jesus in the picture?"

Alan was stunned. He hadn't thought of Jesus being there. Finally he responded, "I guess he's off in the distance somewhere, waiting to see if I get it right."

Like many of us, Alan needs a radical change in his understanding of Jesus! He is present in every circumstance of our lives. When we respond in faith to Jesus' death and resurrection, it makes it possible for God, in the person of the Holy Spirit, to dwell within us. Thus we take him into every situation we enter. His presence is active and always available. He is ready to provide whatever we may need. The resources of God were available to Alan all along, if only he were aware of that divine and loving presence. In this study we will look at the truth that the Holy Spirit was given to assure us that Christ is with us.

"And surely I am with you always."

—matthew 28:20

<u>PREPARING HEART AND MIND</u>

- How has your inner world changed in the last few years?

- In what relationship or situation do you need to be assured that God is with you?

- What keeps you from sinning?

engaging the text

Read John 14:15–27

1. Describe the context of this passage. When, to whom, why, and about what is Jesus talking? (See Setting the Stage.)

2. Jesus implies that, without the Holy Spirit, the disciples are like "orphans" (v. 18). What are some words or phrases that might describe the orphaned state of these disciples (or any non-Christian)?

3. By implication, you, before you received the Holy Spirit, were "orphaned." Describe the evidence in your attitudes, emotions, or behavior that you are no longer an orphan since you became a Christian.

Connect for Life

Most days it was a pleasure to sip coffee at the sidewalk café and watch people pass by. But not this day. A teenager accidentally had tumbled off her bike and fell under a passing tram. In an instant, her leg was severed below the knee. The bloody, broken limb lay beside her, no longer connected to its source of life.

Just like this limb, humanity is separated from the source of life. Paul calls this condition being "dead in our transgression and sins." Apart from Christ, we are all spiritually dead, separated from God. We all have chosen ways to live without him.

If a separated limb were attached to a substitute source of air and nutrients, what good could it do? The image of a leg connected to a life support system seems ridiculous. But that is what we did before connecting to life through faith in Jesus.

Medical workers had little hope of reconnecting the severed limb to the young woman's body. But Jesus is able to unite all of us together with God. When we acknowledge our dead condition and reach out in faith to Jesus, we are connected to the source of life.

What does it mean to have eternal life?

4. What are all the various things said about the Holy Spirit in this passage?

Share an aspect of your own life where you have experienced the work of the Holy Spirit as described in these verses.

5. In verse 20, Jesus says that the disciples will realize the truth that "I am in my Father, and you are in me, and I am in you." How does the Holy Spirit make us certain of this truth?

How does the certainty of this truth affect your daily life?

A Personal Testimony

My world came crashing down when my wife left me for another man—worse yet with another married man from my office. I had invested so much love in her, and now my hopes for the future lay shattered. Yet in my darkest hours of loneliness and pain, I began to sense that God was reaching out to me. It dawned on me that I had placed all my security in a person, and people fail. "But I never fail. I will never leave you or forsake you," said the gentle words that popped into my mind.

For the first time in years, I found myself wanting to go to church. I took a close friend and both of us felt a love that beckoned us to return. The following Sunday both of us gave our hearts to Jesus. I don't remember what the pastor said that day. I only know I became aware of my need for a Savior. I stopped blaming my wife for all my troubles and took responsibility for my own sin.

God's work in me began from the inside out. I didn't feel any emotional rush, only a sense of his Spirit inside me. Old desires began to melt away. New desires replaced them. Desires to draw near to God, to read the Bible, and to fellowship with Christians. It wasn't always easy. During the divorce, I sometimes felt angry and bitter. But the Spirit inside me kept drawing me back, reminding me that I had to let go and trust God. I've had to keep yielding my will to God in the twenty-five years since then. The temptation to sin is always there, but the more I yield to the Spirit, the more I see how empty the enticements of this world are. By following him, I have had joy and blessing beyond my imagination.

6. Why might some people not want to believe this truth?

Read John 16:5–15

7. "It is better to live today with the Holy Spirit in us than to have been one of the original disciples with Jesus." Is this statement true or false? Explain why.

8. Jesus says that the Holy Spirit convicts us of three realities. Identify each of these and explain how each might affect a believer.

9. Choose one of these realities which the Holy Spirit convicts us of. How might your life change if you responded more deeply to his conviction? Be specific.

10. What is Jesus offering to you in verses 12–15, and how can you respond to him?

RESPONDING to GOD

Ask the Holy Spirit to open your eyes to recognize his continual, caring presence and his active involvement in your life.

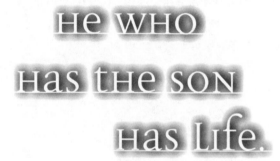

HE WHO HAS THE SON HAS LIFE.

1 John 5:12

taking it further

Suggestions for application

DIGGING DEEPER

For further passages on the giving of the Holy Spirit and the benefits of his presence with us, see:

Matthew 28:20b; Acts 2:38–39; 2 Corinthians 1:21–22; Galatians 3:14; Ephesians 1:13–14.

Connecting to Life

Write out your testimony in about three hundred words, highlighting what took place in your inner world when you accepted Christ as your Savior. Do not focus on your changes of behavior, but on the internal changes of mind and heart. (For those who have been Christians since childhood, it may be more appropriate to contrast changes before and after you began to understand and receive some of the benefits God offers us through the Holy Spirit's indwelling.) For an example, see "A Personal Testimony" on page 17.

Personal Expression

Make a collage of pictures or expressions cut from magazines that show the contrast in your life before and after you began to understand and receive the benefits of the indwelling of the Holy Spirit. Take time to let God encourage you about what he has already done and speak to you about what he may still want to do.

WORLD FOCUS

Using the "Principles for Effective Intercession" on pages 93–4, ask God to show you an individual or nation that needs the gift of life through the Holy Spirit. Take time this week to pray for that person or nation.

BREAKS STRONGHOLDS
Ephesians 1:15–23; 3:14–21

As seven-year-old Ann watched her mother flirting with yet another man at the restaurant, a hot surge of embarrassment pulsed through her body. That day she vowed never to be like her mother.

Ann had not been consciously aware of that vow until a memory of the incident flashed through her mind many years later. She was facing painful questions about her sexual identity and struggling with an eating disorder. Suddenly she realized that her attitude toward being a woman, or at least toward being attractive, had taken a negative turn from the moment of her vow.

Like many of us, Ann had cooperated with lies. Eventually this kind of cooperation leads to sin. The false belief in her case was simply, "It's bad to be an attractive woman." In most cases, lies that feed sinful attitudes and behaviors are rooted in deeply painful experiences. We are not responsible for the sins of those who hurt us. We are, however, responsible for our own reactions to that pain, such as drawing false conclusions about God, ourselves, or life in general.

"You will know the truth, and the truth will set you free."

——JOHN 8:32

The Holy Spirit is a master at exposing and uprooting lies. His first and most fundamental target is the lies which distort our view of God's love for us. The apostle Paul knew this. In his letter to the Ephesian believers, he says he prays constantly that they will cooperate with the Holy Spirit within them, receiving from him the power to overcome lies and grasp the truth. In this study we will learn to pray for the Holy Spirit's work of uprooting lies and establishing truth to be deepened in our lives.

- Satan is called "the deceiver" (2 John 7) and "the father of lies" (John 8:44), not "the greedy one" or "the father of immorality." Why?

- If people were to determine your picture of God from the way you relate to him, what would they conclude?

- How do you know when you are in deception about a certain issue?

engaging the text

Read Ephesians 1:15–23

setting the stage

- The letter to the Ephesians is written to believers, many of whom Paul has personally discipled when he lived among them for about three years.

- It reveals no serious problem of sin in their midst. In fact, it appears that they are maturing in their personal faith and effective in sharing the gospel with the lost.

1. Consider the maturity of the Ephesian believers and identify ways that they might be similar to you (see v. 15 and Setting the Stage).

2. Given that Paul is writing to people who already have a personal relationship with God through the Holy Spirit, what do you think Paul is praying for in verses 16–17, and why?

3. Note that Paul pictures certain aspects of God as he addresses him in prayer. What are some words that you personally associate with "glorious" and "father"?

   • glorious:

   • father:

   How might this concept of God as both "glorious" and our "father" improve your prayer life?

4. In the context of this passage, the "heart" means the mind, will, and emotions. In verses 18–23, identify the three things about which Paul prays that the believers will receive more revelation. Describe what impact that revelation could have on your own heart.

Prayer request	Anticipated heart impact
1.	1.
2.	2.
3.	3.

5. Which of these three elements do you need more understanding of? Explain why.

Read Ephesians 3:14–21

    6. Put verse 16 into your own words. (Remember that Paul is praying for people who are already Christians.)

A Paraphrase of Paul's Prayers

Ephesians 1:17–18:

Dad, no one and nothing is wiser, stronger, or more trustworthy than you. I know that in my head, but sometimes my heart doesn't really grasp this truth. Instead, I act as if you were distant, uncaring, and yet demanding perfection. I need you to adjust my internal process so my thinking about you is accurate and my heart response is consistent with who you really are and who I really am—your beloved child.

Ephesians 1:19–22:

Stopping to tune into my inner world is the most risky thing I do. Listening, facing the reality within, is scary. However, when I do, I discover treasures: truths that only you can speak.

I hear the faint whispers of hope. Turn up the volume. May your voice of hope be so strong that it will echo in my heart like the sound of a Swiss horn in the Alps.

And what's that? You say I am your inheritance? Of all the beauty and value in the created order, you have chosen the likes of me to bring the greatest pleasure to your heart! I am sorry, but that is beyond me. Please convince me.

Daily evil lurks around me, knowing just what to say to throw me into confusion. You offer power, resurrection power, to enable me to stand against this. I need more of it.

7. In verse 17, we see that our response of faith results in Christ dwelling in our hearts. Explain what Paul means by Christ "dwelling" (making his home) in our hearts and why faith is important.

8. If what Paul prays for in verse 16 was answered in your life, how would you be different?

9. Paul implies that we as believers are rooted in love, but that we need power to understand how much we are loved (vv. 17–18). Why do we need power to understand?

10. Identify as many lies as you can that keep people from believing in God's love for them.

Standing Up to the Father of Lies

The contrast between Jesus and Satan shows why our mind is such a battlefield. Jesus is the truth, the giver of abundant life. Satan is the father of all lies who comes to rob us of life. From the first conflict in the Garden of Eden, Satan's strategy has been to distort the truth and lead us to question God's Word. Satan didn't need to demonstrate his power to Adam and Eve. Simply believing his lies led to their spiritual death.

We also are vulnerable to the enemy's clever mixtures of truth and deception. The pages of history reflect the variety of ideologies that Satan has used to cause people to doubt God. Sometimes these false ideologies deny the existence of God; sometimes they distort his true nature. In every case, they lead to a devaluation of man, creation, art, morals, and knowledge.

Thankfully, Satan does not have the last word. Jesus' sacrificial death has disarmed Satan's power over us. If we cling to the truth (what God says about himself), we can stand up to the father of lies and be guaranteed to win!

What lies has Satan used to undermine your faith? Combat them by immersing yourself in the Scriptures. Think through how you can get more of God's Word into your life.

11. Which of these lies do you recognize as part of your own distorted perspective of God's love?

12. In 2 Corinthians 10:4, Paul indicates that God's inspired Word tears down strongholds, or false beliefs. What role do you think the Holy Spirit plays in relation to tearing down these false beliefs?

13. Identify several passages of Scripture which affirm God's love for you and which you can refer to in the future, as you invite the Holy Spirit to reveal their truths to your heart and mind.

RESPONDING to GOD

Invite Christ to increase in every aspect of your being, so that your mind, emotions, and will are more responsive to him. Ask particularly for the Holy Spirit's power to overcome any lies you identified in your life when you answered Question 11. Pray that instead of those lies, you will be filled more and more with the truth and presence of God.

the one who
is in you
is greater than
the one who is
in the world.

1 John 4:4

taking it further

Suggestions for application

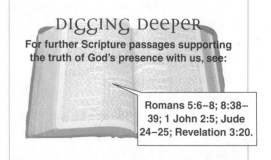

DIGGING DEEPER

For further Scripture passages supporting the truth of God's presence with us, see:

Romans 5:6–8; 8:38–39; 1 John 2:5; Jude 24–25; Revelation 3:20.

Personal Expression

Draw a picture or create a collage that illustrates what the Holy Spirit promises to do for your heart.

Connecting to Life

Read "Standing Up to the Father of Lies" on page 29 and answer the question: What lies has Satan used to undermine your faith? Combat them by immersing yourself in the Scriptures. Think through how you can get more of God's Word into your life.

Meditation

Rewrite Paul's prayer for the Ephesians in your own words, being sure to make it personal. (For an example of this, see "A Paraphrase of Paul's Prayers" on page 27.) Pray this for yourself and for others that you care about.

Reveals the Word
Luke 24:1–32, 45

George Müller began a ministry that rescued hundreds of starving orphans from death in the slums of England. As important as his role was in showing these needy children the love of their heavenly Father, the ministry was never Müller's first priority. He believed the highest call on his life was an intimate relationship with God, which he nurtured through meditating daily on God's Word.

The concept of meditation comes from a Latin word, *ruminare*, that describes a cow chewing the cud. The grass is eaten, chewed, swallowed, regurgitated, chewed some more, and swallowed again. This process depends on digestive juices to break the food down into a form the body can absorb. Applying this analogy to meditation, the grass is like God's Word and the juices are like the Holy Spirit who helps us to "digest" the Word. As we slowly and deliberately consider Scripture, allowing the Holy Spirit to work, he breaks it down and applies it to our lives. Our hearts and minds are nourished and strengthened.

> **"Were not our hearts burning within us while he ... opened the Scriptures to us?"**
>
> **——Luke 24:32**

If only the disciples had meditated regularly on what Jesus had said to them before he died! Amazingly, in the midst of the traumatic events surrounding his death and resurrection, they forgot them.

In this study we look at the process Jesus leads his disciples through after his resurrection. He graciously brings them to the place of revelation concerning the truth about himself. Whatever challenging and unexpected circumstances you may find yourself in, the Holy Spirit can do for you what Jesus does for his disciples in Luke 24.

PREPARING heart anD mIND

- Describe the difference between head knowledge and heart knowledge.

- When you spend time reading the Bible, what would help you to better hear God speak to your heart?

- In Luke 24, Jesus asks the two disciples questions that cause them to put their thoughts and doubts into words. What thought-provoking questions might Jesus be asking you at present?

engaging the text

Read Luke 24:1–32, 45

setting the stage

- The women who go to the tomb are followers of Jesus and have experienced firsthand his ministry and teaching (Luke 8:1–3).

- Peter has had at least one intense talk with Jesus regarding his death and resurrection (Matthew 16:13–28).

- "How foolish you are . . ." In this culture, these are not considered harsh or condescending words but straightforward talk. The two disciples would not be insulted by them.

1. Jesus has just been crucified and buried. If you were one of his disciples, what would you have needed to know in order to face the crucifixion with faith and hope?

2. Given how familiar the disciples are with Jesus' ministry, how is it possible that both the women and Peter seem to have forgotten (see verses 1–12) what Jesus has told them (see Setting the Stage)?

3. Think of a difficult situation in your life at present. How would it change if you "remembered," or applied, the truth of the cross and resurrection?

4. What do you think keeps the two on the way to Emmaus from recognizing Jesus? (Note: the answer includes several elements.)

Remember What You're Worth!

Mandy could hardly believe the tragic TV news report. A man whose home was threatened by a raging fire had escaped the flames but run back in to rescue his cat. The fire trapped and killed him. As she finished the breakfast dishes, Mandy wondered if the man could do it over, would he take that risk again? Surely his life was worth more than the cat's.

Just then another scene played out in Mandy's mind. Jesus was being asked if he had the option, would he die for her again? In that moment, the thought of Jesus choosing to die to save her seemed as ridiculous as a man choosing to die to save his cat. Mandy was astonished when she felt she heard Jesus say, "Yes, she is worth it."

What determines the value of something? Isn't it simply what someone is willing to pay for it? In the true story above, the pet owner was willing to risk his own life for the cat. In reality, God gave his Son for you. He would have died for you, even if no one else believed in him but you.

Jesus' life is the value God puts on you. If you truly believed you are that valuable, what would change in the way you think or act?

5. Describe the process that leads them out of disillusionment to vision (vv. 13–30). Note the interaction between Jesus and the two disciples (see Setting the Stage).

6. What do we learn about Jesus as we see how he responds to those who are doubting?

7. What is most meaningful to you personally in Jesus' responses? Why?

8. As with these two disciples, Jesus is walking beside you even now. What might be keeping you from "seeing" him? Why?

9. The two invite Jesus into their home to continue their fellowship. (Jesus would not have forced his way in.) Identify a time, after you became a Christian, when you invited Jesus' presence (the Holy Spirit) into an area of your life (such as a relationship, a decision, a fear, your finances). What was the result?

A Truth Beyond Reason

When Paul says in 2 Timothy 3:16, "All Scripture is God-breathed," he is affirming that every line is infused with the very life of God. The Bible is God's self-revelation. It allows an understanding of truth that cannot be achieved solely on the basis of human reason and inquiry.

Our human faculty of reason is simply insufficient for understanding God, ourselves, or the world around us. We need God. His Holy Spirit enables us to understand and obey Scripture (1 John 2:27). And when we affirm that the Bible is his inspired Word, we open ourselves up to the ultimate source of insight and truth.

Through this divinely inspired communication, we discover the very character and nature of God. Whenever we read, study, memorize, or meditate on the Word of God, our objective should be to know him better. A desire for a growing friendship with God should keep us coming back to the Scriptures again and again until we are "thoroughly equipped for every good work" (2 Timothy 3:17).

What do you need understanding for? Ask God, search his Word for insight, and listen to the Holy Spirit.

10. Describe in your own words what Jesus does for the disciples in verses 8, 27, 32, and 45.

11. What might the connection be between the condition of a person's heart and that person's ability to really understand God's Word?

12. What do you personally do at present to receive insight from the Holy Spirit when you read the Scriptures?

RESPONDING to GOD

Invite the Holy Spirit to open your eyes to the reality of his Word, just as Jesus did for the two disciples.

THE WORD OF GOD . . .
IS AT WORK
IN YOU
WHO BELIEVE.

1 Thessalonians 2:13

taking it further

Suggestions for application

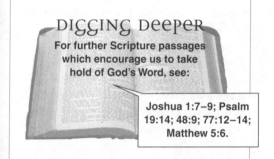

DIGGING DEEPER

For further Scripture passages which encourage us to take hold of God's Word, see:

Joshua 1:7–9; Psalm 19:14; 48:9; 77:12–14; Matthew 5:6.

Meditation

Read Galatians 2:20: "I have been crucified with Christ and I no longer live, but Christ lives in me. The life I live in the body, I live by faith in the Son of God, who loved me and gave himself for me." Ask God three questions about the text (for example, "What does it mean to be crucified with Christ?). Take time to dialogue with God about them.

Connecting to Life

Read "Remember What You're Worth!" on page 36 then respond to the following: Jesus' life is the value God puts on you. If you truly believed you are that valuable, what would change in the way you think or act?

WORLD FOCUS

Read the "People Profile" about the Wolof on the next two pages and take time to pray for them in the coming week. You may also find it helpful to refer to the "Principles for Effective Intercession" on pages 93–4.

PEOPLE PROFILE

the Wolof—Jesus, the Perfect Griot

Location: Senegal. Population: 2.9 million. Religion: 99% Muslim.

Expectancy filled the air. Wolof children stared wide-eyed, and adults hardly breathed. Even the chickens stopped their scratching and cackling. The *griot* (storyteller) had the villagers straining to catch every word.

Skill and wisdom with the spoken word marks a Wolof as a person of maturity, as one who commands respect. Parents encourage their children to memorize the hundreds of Wolof proverbs, to invent secret languages, and to develop their verbal skills through storytelling, riddles, and poetry. The power of the spoken word captures and dominates Wolof thinking.

Far away, long ago, another *griot* captured the crowd's attention with stories of houses built on rocks, shepherds seeking lost sheep, and widows giving their pennies. Intent on the storyteller, the Jews sat as quietly as the Wolof to hear words skillfully woven into the fabric of the tale. Jesus was not only bringing God's Word, he *was* God's Word. "In the beginning was the Word, and the Word was with God, and the Word was God" (John 1:1): Jesus, the living Word of God. Jesus, the perfect *griot*. Jesus, the perfect man of wisdom and maturity. Jesus, the perfect Wolof.

Pray that:

- The Holy Spirit would reveal Jesus as the perfect Wolof man, destroying their view of him as a "foreign" Jesus.
- God would astonish and capture the Wolof imagination with Jesus, the living Word of God.
- The Wolof would begin to "gossip" about Jesus to each other in their stories, parables, and riddles.
- Influential Wolof men and women would point others to the living Word.
- Powerful evangelistic, storytelling ministries would be raised up for the Wolof.

WHISPERS TO US ABOUT THE FATHER
Luke 15:11–32; Romans 8:15–16

A horrifying earthquake rumbled through Armenia on a wintry December day in 1988. Buildings shattered and over fifty thousand residents died in the course of a few minutes. One father ran to the school where his son was a student but found it crushed to rubble. He immediately began digging. Hour after hour he searched for signs of life. Others gave up, declaring that there was no hope of finding anyone else alive. But the father kept digging, his hands bleeding. More than thirty-six hours later, he heard a faint voice. He broke through the stones to find his son and thirteen other students huddled together in a small air pocket. "I told them you would find us, Father," cried the tearful boy. "I knew you wouldn't give up."

God sent the Spirit of his Son into our hearts, . . . who calls out, "*Abba*, Father."

—GALATIANS 4:6

Even greater than that earthly father's love is the love our heavenly Father has for us. He does not give up on us either. In this study, we focus on the truth of God's Father heart toward us. Learn to listen to the Holy Spirit's constant whisper to your heart about God's unconditional love for you.

PREPARING HEART AND MIND

- How would one know if one's image of God is distorted?

- How do you know when the Holy Spirit is speaking to you?

- Think of some physical object, no bigger than a shoe box, that symbolizes for you some aspect of God's Father heart toward you. Explain why.

engaging the text

setting the stage

- In the time of Jesus, the Jewish people do not see God as a loving Father who wants a relationship with his children.

- Jesus teaches God's love for us through his parables and models it in his own relationship with the Father. But even Jesus is limited in communicating this truth because of the powers of darkness blinding people.

- In defeating those powers on the cross, he made way for the Holy Spirit to be given so that he, the Master of truth, could reveal God's Father heart to believers.

Read Luke 15:11–32

1. Many characteristics of the father in this parable are also true of God. Identify them and explain how they are similar to qualities of God.

2. Compare the younger son's image of his father with that of the older son's image.

3. Which son do you think is most like you? Explain why.

4. What are some words that you associate with the phrase, "intimacy with God"?

Intimacy Is a Choice

One of the most amazing aspects of our friendship with God is his respect for our boundaries. He does not impose himself, his gifts, or his will on us. He lets us choose. He honors our "yes" and our "no"—even when our choices hurt ourselves and others, including God himself.

This principle is illustrated in the story of the lost son. The older son chose to work in the field, in close proximity to his father, but the resentment he later expressed showed that he had needs he did not allow his father to meet. The father respected his distance. By contrast, the younger son approached his father to ask for something potentially harmful. The father trusted him and gave to him what he asked. When the younger son returned, broken and repentant, he moved toward his father for help. Once again, the father responded.

Unfortunately, the bitter older son kept his distance. What a tragedy. This son did not open up to his father.

The quality of our friendship with God is affected by our choice to approach him, to open ourselves to him, and to receive from him what we need.

Describe your relationship with God the Father. Are you able to approach him and receive from him?

5. Analyze each of the relationships below in terms of levels of intimacy.

- Father with younger son

- Father with older son

- Older son with younger son

6. Describe your own experience of intimacy with God, or your lack of it.

7. How do you think your image of God might affect your level of intimacy with him?

Risking Friendship with God

Leigh's spiked hair, torn black clothes, and nose ring made her different from the other young people at the church youth group. Her tough posture signaled to them that she had no intention of getting close to anyone, especially not God. She had been abused too many times. She was certain that God would reject her, too, once he got to know her. So it wasn't long before she left the youth group.

Intimate friendship with God is risky for many. Some, like Leigh, have learned to survive alone, keeping God at a distance. Others, who believe that acceptance is earned through performance, feel they must work hard for God's friendship. The fact that God loves us, no matter what we look like, where we come from, or what we do, is beyond human understanding.

God knows our struggle to grasp this reality. He gently takes the initiative in the friendship. His Spirit continually reveals his true nature to us (Ephesians 1:17–19). He repeatedly assures us that he is with us and will never leave us.

8. Which quality of God, reflected in this parable, do you want to understand better, and why?

Read Romans 8:15–16

9. According to these verses, what does the Holy Spirit do and with what result?

10. Describe any awareness you have of the inner voice of the Holy Spirit talking to your heart about the Father.

Invite the Holy Spirit to open your ears and heart to hear more clearly his whispers about the Father.

perfect love

drives out

fear.

1 John 4:18

taking it further
Suggestions for application

DIGGING DEEPER

For further Scriptures about God's love and commitment, see:

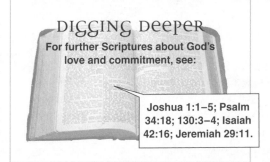

Joshua 1:1–5; Psalm 34:18; 130:3–4; Isaiah 42:16; Jeremiah 29:11.

Personal Expression

Pictures of the Father: Cut out pictures or words from magazines and/or use small objects to make a collage that depicts truth that you want to know about the Father. Invite the Holy Spirit into the process and let him speak to you through it.

Connecting to Life

Read "Intimacy Is a Choice" on page 46, then answer the following: Describe your relationship with God the Father. Are you able to approach him and receive from him?

WORLD FOCUS

Pray for Muslim peoples to recognize God's Father heart toward them and his free gift of grace to them in Jesus. The "Principles for Effective Intercession" on pages 93–94 may be helpful.

RESTRAINS PASSION
1 Samuel 25:1–42

The horse-drawn carriage entered the park lane, the lovely bride seated within. The roads were wet and muddy from a recent rainstorm, slowing down the journey to the church. Suddenly, "Stop!" cried the bride, and, leaping from her seat, she plunged into the mud beside the carriage. A passerby scowled at her. "What do you think you're doing?" he snorted. "You're nothing but a mud-loving tramp!" The bride seemed to agree as she continued to run fistfuls of mud through her hair.

At length another voice reached her ears. "Miss, Miss, you don't belong in that mud!" Slowly she turned and, looking up, saw the carriage driver reaching out to help her. "Don't you remember you're a bride? Your groom is waiting for you!" At last the truth of his words penetrated her heart. She was not a tramp but a beloved bride! She drew herself up and stepped into the carriage, leaving the mud and filth behind.

But you are . . . chosen . . . royal . . . holy.

—1 PETER 2:9

Of course, this story is too ridiculous to be real—or is it? Think about it. This incredible tale illustrates a powerful biblical truth that runs through the Scriptures. When we give in to a temptation to sin, it's as if we throw ourselves into the mud, losing sight of how God sees us and loves us. The best safeguards against sin are a clear focus on God and a strong relationship with him. The Holy Spirit, who is in each of us as believers, faithfully reminds us of these things. When we grasp the truth, seeing ourselves as set apart for a loving and holy God, sin no longer holds its appeal.

There is an interesting parallel to this in David's life, involving a wealthy man named Nabal and his wife, Abigail. David, in the heat of his anger, is intent on committing murder until Abigail intervenes. How she interacts with David to turn him from sin is a concrete illustration of how the Holy Spirit interacts with a believer in similar circumstances.

As we study this passage, be listening as the Holy Spirit reminds you of who you are in Christ.

PREPARING HEART AND MIND

- When are you most sensitive to the Holy Spirit's voice—before, during, or after you sin?

- Consider the statement: "I think of myself more as a person who is vulnerable to sin than someone who has been set apart for God." Is this true or false for you? Why?

- The secret to self-control is . . .

engaging the text

setting the stage

- In David's time, generosity toward strangers is normal and expected at festival times especially.

- Sheep-shearing time is considered a time of festivity and sharing.

- Jesus often uses everyday situations as parables to illustrate spiritual truths, and we are looking at this true-life story in a similar way.

Read 1 Samuel 25:1–42

1. On what grounds does David ask for provisions from Nabal? (See verses 7–8, 14–17, 21, and Setting the Stage.)

2. Describe David's attitude toward Nabal at this point (vv. 7–8).

3. What about Nabal's response would be upsetting to David and why (vv. 10–17)?

4. How would you be tempted to react if someone offended you in a similar way?

Cut to the Heart

Maria had been lying to her parents for years, mostly about little things she considered insignificant. But since she'd become a Christian, a strange thing was happening. She felt a twinge of conscience each time she was tempted to lie. She also began to see for the first time the impact of earlier deceptions, and she was feeling a need to ask for forgiveness.

As in Maria's case, the Holy Spirit brings us conviction of sin. Sometimes we may confuse his work with Satan's condemnation. Here are some distinguishing marks that will help us discern the difference:

Condemnation	*Conviction*
Comes from Satan	Comes from God
Is vague, general	Is specific, concrete
Leads to hopelessness, no way out	Gives hope, practical steps to solution
Comes with destructive insults	Comes with affirmations of love
Should be rejected	Should be embraced

5. What stops David from sinning (vv. 14–35)?

6. What stops you from sinning?

7. Put into your own words what Abigail says to David (vv. 24–31).

8. Why do Abigail's actions and words stop David?

9. Think of how the Holy Spirit has functioned in your life in a similar manner to the way that Abigail functions here for David. Describe how he does it.

The Voice of Righteousness

Nabal had responded contemptuously to David's simple request for some provisions. David reacted quickly and apparently with violent intentions. What stopped him from succumbing to this great temptation to sin? The truthful, timely words of Abigail. She reminded David of God's promises to him and encouraged him to count the cost of the action he was about to take.

Similarly, the Holy Spirit speaks to our hearts in the midst of temptation. Through the voice of friends or through his own voice, he reminds us of God's promises to us and the truth that we are the "temple of the Holy Spirit" (1 Corinthians 6:19). God has equipped us with a conscience to guide us into doing right and to alarm us when we have sinned.

We can harden our hearts or sear our conscience (1 Timothy 4:2) by repeated disobedience. On the other hand, our "spiritual ears" can become more responsive to the Holy Spirit as we learn to hear the truth and obey.

HOT topic

Addiction can be defined as being caught in a sinful habit or pattern of behavior. Choose the statement below that you most agree with and defend it.

"Addiction is a humanistic excuse for sin. One can always say no to sin."

"Addiction is a real state which can only be broken by walking through a process with God."

10. In 1 Corinthians 10:13, Paul says, "No temptation has seized you except what is common to man. And God is faithful; he will not let you be tempted beyond what you can bear. But when you are tempted, he will also provide a way out so that you can stand up under it." How does God provide a way out for someone who is being tempted?

11. In the heat of the moment, what can we do to listen to the Holy Spirit as David listens to Abigail?

A sk the Holy Spirit to open your ears to hear him in the midst of temptation.

THE ONE WHO
IS IN YOU
IS GREATER THAN
THE ONE WHO IS
IN THE WORLD.

1 John 4:4

taking it further

Suggestions for application

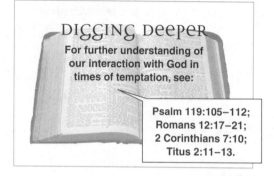

DIGGING DEEPER

For further understanding of our interaction with God in times of temptation, see:

Psalm 119:105–112;
Romans 12:17–21;
2 Corinthians 7:10;
Titus 2:11–13.

WORLD FOCUS

Pray for a nation to turn from their sin to God. Ask God to tell you which one to pray for. "Prayer Strategies for Changing Nations" (pages 95–97) could be helpful as you pray.

Meditation

Using 3 x 5 cards, write out truths that you have learned or been reminded of concerning:

- the Holy Spirit's involvement in your life.
- who you are in Christ.

Use one card for each phrase. Put the cards by your mirror, on your desk, or any place you see daily. For the remainder of this study on the Holy Spirit, focus on one card each day.

Connecting to Life

Read "Cut to the Heart" on page 55 then answer the following: Compare a time when you experienced conviction with a time when you experienced condemnation. Discuss the difference.

Satisfies Our Heart
John 4:1–27

Doreen looked stunning in her new short skirt and jacket, and she knew it. Several men in the room smiled or winked at her, and she was trying to decide which one she wanted. She drank in the attention as if she had just reached an oasis after days of hot, dusty travel through a barren desert. She was not about to settle for just one man but was going to make the most of this. Sadly, no one saw beyond the attractive facade to her empty, thirsty heart, not even Doreen herself.

Jesus understands the deep longings of the human heart. He made us with needs for intimacy that only he could meet. Like Doreen, many of us attempt to meet these needs through substitutes such as money, sex, religion, or work. But ultimately only Jesus can satisfy. He is the living water. Pure spring water strengthens and refreshes our bodies. Some substitutes we use may taste good for the moment,

"If anyone is thirsty, let him come to me and drink."

—JOHN 7:37

but slowly their toxins poison our system. If Doreen had let Jesus quench her inner thirst for intimacy with his abounding love, her unhealthy longing for men's attention would have soon diminished.

In this study we look at Jesus' interaction with a needy woman like Doreen. The water he offers her is the same living water he offers to us today through his gift of the Holy Spirit. Are you aware of this living water running deep within you? Ask the Holy Spirit to open up your heart to drink in more of his presence, his love, and his truth as you go through this study.

PREPARING HEART AND MIND

- "I have never known a time when I have not felt emptiness inside me." How true is this statement for you?

- When are you content?

- In what ways do you avoid silence or solitude? Why?

engaging the text

setting the stage

- The sixth hour is noon, the hottest part of the day. People do not normally come to the well when the sun is at its hottest.

- This well is known to contain living, natural spring water, not rainwater.

- In this culture, receiving a guest to your land and offering hospitality is considered a citizen's responsibility.

- Samaritans are half Jewish and despised by the Jews. Most Jews traveling from Jerusalem to Galilee would take a longer path to avoid Samaria.

- It is not acceptable for men and women to interact socially in this culture.

Read John 4:1–27

1. Describe the woman in this story. (Who is she? Who are her friends and family? What has been her contribution to those in her society? See Setting the Stage.)

2. What or whom might she be avoiding, and why? (See Setting the Stage.)

3. The Samaritan woman appears to have been filling a void in her life through relationships with men. In what way(s) do you attempt to fill an inner void?

4. Jesus does several things that surprise both the woman and his disciples. What does he do and why?

5. What aspect of Jesus' interaction with the woman is most meaningful to you? Why?

6. In verses 10–14, Jesus provokes the woman into thinking about who he is and what he has to offer her. What does he want her to understand about himself and his gift to her?

Thirsty No More

Sharon had heard about Jesus many times. She believed there was a God. She even believed that Jesus lived, died, and rose again. But she could not believe that God would ever forgive her for running away from home, leaving her young children motherless. Whenever she even thought about God, she felt condemned.

She still felt that way as she lay dying from cancer. Then two women came to her hospital bed and talked to her about Jesus again. They explained that Jesus' love for her had motivated him to pay the penalty for her guilt when he died on the cross. They assured her that he was now waiting in heaven to welcome her, if she would only believe.

The voice of condemnation had drowned out that truth so many times before. This time she recognized that Jesus had looked her enemy in the eye, met the demands of the law, canceled her debt, and set her free. That day Jesus became her Savior, her life, even as she breathed her last breath.

What negative thoughts, feelings, or habits do you experience that are rooted in your past? Ask God to set you free on the basis of what Jesus accomplished for you on the cross.

7. Read John 7:37–39, which tells us that the Holy Spirit is the source of living water. What is your understanding and experience of this living water?

Giving Honor to God

Many of us think of worship as what we do on Sunday mornings in church: singing hymns or songs, reading Scripture, standing and kneeling, and praying. But these things are just outward expressions of worship. We can sing beautiful songs to God, but if our lives don't reflect our love for him, our words will be empty.

Four aspects of worship are emphasized in Jesus' teaching in John 4. First, *God is spirit.* Knowing God is the beginning of worship. When we understand how good and how loving he is, it frees us to express our love and emotions to him. *And his worshipers.* A true worshiper is sold out to God, willing to say, "I belong to God. I will obey him no matter what." *Must worship in spirit.* Jesus declared that the place or the method of worship wasn't as important as the act of touching God in one's spirit. True worship is a Spirit-led response to God—to all that he is and all that he has done and is doing and will do. *And in truth.* Finally, Jesus proclaimed that the Father is looking for a special kind of worshiper, one who responds to God's truth and is genuine in responding to him.

Throughout the Bible we read how God's people are strengthened, healed, and delivered as they worship. It's still happening today. Communion with an awesome God, perfect in love and holiness, transforms us.

8. What is the point Jesus is making about worship in verses 21–24?

9. What do you think the connection is between worship and experiencing the "living water" of the Spirit?

10. How might worship become more a part of your daily experience?

Invite the Holy Spirit to lead you to drink more of this living water.

engaging in true worship satisfies the deepest human longings.

taking it further

Suggestions for application

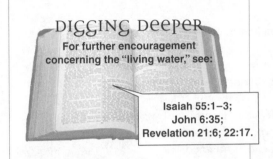

DIGGING DEEPER

For further encouragement concerning the "living water," see:

Isaiah 55:1–3;
John 6:35;
Revelation 21:6; 22:17.

Meditation

Prayerfully listen to a worship tape. As you listen, write out a list of words or phrases that describe why God is worthy of your worship.

Connecting to Life

Identify one person you know who needs to experience this living water. Ask God what step you can take this week toward that person.

WORLD FOCUS

Read the People Profile about the Kyrgyz of South Central Asia on page 70. In the coming week, take time to pray that they will come to know the living water of Jesus and be freed from shame. (See "Principles for Effective Intercession" on pages 93–4 to help you.)

PEOPLE PROFILE

the kyrgyz — burdened by shame

Location: Kyrgyzstan, Russia, Uzbekistan, China. Population: 2.9 million. Religion: 75% Muslim.

Aibek lowered his eyes as he walked by the other *yurts* (tents). Conversation died as he passed the group of women milking goats and the men catching the early morning sun. His face reddened by *ooyat* (shame), he quickly disappeared into the *yurt*, relieved to be hidden from the gaze of the other families.

Gossip had spread quickly through the *yaylaou* (yurt encampment). The name of Aibek's son, Daniar, and the refrain *"ooyat, ooyat"* were whispered in hushed and shocked tones. Daniar had publicly humiliated the *aqsaqal* (chief elder). Before the whole community Daniar had spoken arrogantly and disrespectfully to the *aqsaqal*. He had rejected the *aqsaqal's* authority, turned his back, and walked away. Even his uncles had trouble restraining Daniar. The damage he had done seemed beyond repair. Daniar had brought shame upon himself and his whole family. They now felt naked, vulnerable, and ashamed to be seen by others in the community. Until Aibek could find a way to remove the shame, he and his family would be condemned to hide in self-imposed exile.

At the dawn of time another man rejected the authority of his *aqsaqal*. Like Daniar, he and his family had to live with the shame that resulted. Adam disobeyed his heavenly *Aqsaqal* (the Lord God), rejected his words, and went his own way. Adam quickly became aware of his nakedness and shame and hid himself from God.

On the cross, Jesus Christ, God's one and only Son, took our guilt, dealing forever with the problem of sin. Yet the cross was more than just a solution for our guilt. Jesus hung on the cross, bearing the shame of mankind (Hebrew 12:2).

Aibek has no idea that Jesus has already provided a solution for our shame. The Kyrgyz center their lives around avoiding shame. To be called "shameful" by a fellow Kyrgyz is one of the greatest insults in their culture.

Pray that:

- The Kyrgyz would come to know that "anyone who trusts in [Jesus] will never be put to shame" (Romans 10:11).
- Christians would find meaningful ways to explain that Jesus has provided an answer to both guilt and shame.
- The Kyrgyz would recognize Jesus as their heavenly Aqsaqal.

Leader's Notes

Leading a Bible study — especially for the first time — can make you feel both nervous and excited. If you are nervous, realize that you are in good company. Many biblical leaders, such as Moses, Joshua, and the apostle Paul, felt nervous and inadequate to lead others (see, for example, 1 Corinthians 2:3). Yet God's grace was sufficient for them, just as it will be for you.

Some excitement is also natural. Your leadership is a gift to the others in the group. Keep in mind, however, that other group members also share responsibility for the group. Your role is simply to stimulate discussion by asking questions and encouraging people to respond. The suggestions below can help you to be an effective leader.

The Role of the Holy Spirit

Always remember that the work of the Holy Spirit is necessary in order for each of us to understand and apply God's Word. Prayer, your prayer for one another, is critical for revelation to take place. You can be assured that God is working in every group member's life. Look for what is stirring in people's hearts. Listen to their statements and questions, and be aware of what they do not say as well as what they do say. Watch God do his work. He will help you lead others and feed you at the same time. May God's blessing be with you.

Preparing to Lead

1. Ask God to help you understand and apply the passage to your own life. Unless this happens, you will not be prepared to lead others.

2. Carefully work through each question in the study guide. Meditate and reflect on the passage as you formulate your answers.
3. Familiarize yourself with the leader's notes for the session. These will help you understand the purpose of the session and will provide valuable information about the questions.
4. Pray for the various members of the group. Ask God to use these studies to help you grow as disciples of Jesus Christ.
5. Before each meeting, make sure each person has a study guide. Encourage them to prepare beforehand for each study.

Leading the Study

Opening (approximately 5 minutes)

1. At the beginning of your first time together, take a little extra time to explain that the Living Encounters are designed for discussions, sharing, and prayer together, not as lectures. Encourage everyone to participate, but realize that some may be hesitant to speak during the first few sessions.
2. Begin on time. If people realize that the study begins on schedule, they will work harder to arrive on time. Open in prayer. You may then want to ask for feedback from one person who has followed through on the "Taking It Further" section from the previous week's study.
3. Read the introduction together. This will orient the group to the passage being studied.

Preparing Heart and Mind (approximately 15 minutes)

1. Although these questions may be considered by individuals beforehand, you are strongly encouraged to begin your group time with them. They are designed to provoke thinking about a topic that is directly related to the study. Anyone who wrestles with one or more of the questions will be better prepared to receive the truth found in the rest of the study.

2. If your time is very limited, encourage your group members to consider one or more of the questions before they arrive. It is not necessary to mention them in your meeting. However, you may want to ask for one person who has already considered the questions to share thoughts about one question with the group before moving on to "Engaging the Text."

Engaging the Text (approximately 50 minutes)

1. This section is a study of one or more passages of Scripture. Read the Scripture portion(s) aloud. You may choose to do this yourself, or you might ask for volunteers.
2. There are normally 10–12 questions, which will take the group through an inductive process of looking at the text. These questions are designed to be used just as they are written. If you wish, you may simply read each one aloud. Or you may prefer to express a question in your own words until it is clearly understood. Unnecessary rewording, however, is not recommended.
3. Don't be afraid of silence. People in the group may need time to think before responding.
4. Avoid answering your own questions. Even an eager group will quickly become passive and silent if they think the leader will do most of the talking.
5. Encourage more than one answer to each question. Ask, "What do the rest of you think?" or, "Anyone else?" until several people have had a chance to respond.
6. Try to be affirming whenever possible. Let people know you appreciate their insights into the passage.
7. Never reject an answer. If it is clearly wrong, ask, "Which verse led you to that conclusion?" Or let the group handle the problem by asking them what they think about the question.

8. Avoid going off on tangents. If people wander off course, gently bring them back to the passage being considered.
9. End on time. This will be easier if you control the pace of the discussion by not spending too much time on some questions or too little on others.

Articles

There are several articles in each study that are set off by gray boxes. These offer additional information as well as help to liven up the group time. "Setting the Stage" relates directly to the study of the passage, and questions will refer you to this sidebar when needed. Other gray-boxed articles can further illustrate or apply a principle. Become acquainted with the articles beforehand so that you know what is available. Remember that reading one or more of these articles in the group will add to your meeting time.

Responding to God (approximately 10 minutes)

In every study guide a prayer response is built into the last few minutes of the group time. This is to allow for the Holy Spirit to bring further revelation as well as application of the truths studied into each person's life. Usually there is a suggested way to respond in prayer, but feel free to adjust that as you sense what God is doing.

Taking It Further

You may want to encourage people to do one or more of these suggestions during the week ahead. Perhaps ask one person to share about it at your next time together. Or, depending on your time constraints, you may choose to do some of these activities during your session together.

Many more suggestions and helps are found in the book *Leading Bible Discussions* (InterVarsity Press). Reading it would be well worth your time.

SESSION ONE

ASSURES US OF HIS PRESENCE
John 14:15–27; 16:5–15

Purpose: To help people to become more aware of the life of the Holy Spirit, who has been within them from the moment they put their faith in Jesus Christ.

Engaging the Text

Question 1 Jesus is speaking to those who have followed him closely. He is preparing them for his departure and the coming of the Holy Spirit, who will be given to them once he returns to the Father.

Question 3 Some group members may have difficulty answering this question and will perhaps need some prompting. It may be helpful to ask what motivated or drove a person before coming to Christ and how that has now changed. Often people "masked" the emptiness or loneliness they had felt before conversion without acknowledging the feelings behind their behavior. These masks can be: the misuse of substances such as alcohol, food, or drugs; or addictive relationships; or work, sports, achievement, and so on. Attitudes and emotions people may have had can include such things as pessimism, hopelessness, bitterness. Of course, these attitudes, emotions, and behaviors may still exist after coming to Christ. The aim of this study is to help people understand that they can experience God at a deeper level than they are perhaps aware of now, and that he *can* bring about change.

Question 4a The most significant point is that the Holy Spirit is "in" us, and that he gives assurances that he is "in" us. He also comforts, brings life, and gives reassurance that he is with us.

Question 5 It is important to grasp the fact that God intends *all* Christians individually to know the reality of the Holy Spirit at work in their hearts and lives. Be sure to encourage people to share how they experience this personally.

Question 6 Those who have had little experience of healthy, loving primary relationships (family, authority, spouse) usually resist intimacy with God, as it is hard for them to trust anyone. Even as Christians, having received the Holy Spirit, they do not want to risk receiving his love, out of fear of losing it. Others would rather live independently from God, and being reminded that he is with them wherever they go is inconvenient.

Question 7 This is true (see 16:7). The disciples had Jesus with them as an example to follow, but the power of sin and death had not yet been broken (on the cross). Nor had the disciples received the internal resources of God, through the Holy Spirit, to instruct them and empower them to do God's will.

Question 8 The Holy Spirit convicts of sin, righteousness, and judgment.

1. Conviction of sin helps believers see sin from God's perspective and helps us know when something is wrong and needs to be dealt with.

2. Conviction of righteousness helps believers keep in mind that God is holy and that they have been "set apart" (made holy). God now dwells within them. A believer with this reality clearly in mind is less likely to slip into sin.

3. Conviction or certainty that the evil one has been judged reminds believers of God's justice and that payment is necessary

for all evil, both that committed against them and that committed by them. People are also reassured that God is greater than
the evil one.

Question 10 Jesus offers us the Holy Spirit, who works in us in such a way
that everything Jesus said, and all he did for us on the cross,
can be applied in our hearts and lives. Thus through him we
experience such gifts as forgiveness, freedom from sin and
condemnation, and instruction and empowerment to do God's
will. In fact, Jesus says that the Holy Spirit will make available
to us everything that the Father is and all he has to give us.

Taking It Further

Refer to the explanation of this section in the introduction to the Leader's
Notes. While not a requirement, the aim of these suggestions is to help the
study have a continuing effect on lives through the following week.
Encourage people to choose one or more of the activities which appeal to
them. Make it clear that they are not expected to follow through on all the
suggestions.

session two

Breaks Strongholds
Ephesians 1:15–23; 3:14–21

Purpose: For people to be made aware of the need for more of God to penetrate their mind and heart, replacing lies with truth. Group members learn to activate the work of the Holy Spirit's life through prayer, particularly the kind of prayer Paul prays in his letter to the Ephesians.

Engaging the Text

Question 1   Even though the Ephesians are mature Christians, they still need a work of the Holy Spirit in their lives in order to know God better and to understand better what they have received from him.

Question 2   Paul is praying for them to get to know God better through the ministry of the Holy Spirit.

Question 3   A person who clearly sees God as big, worthy, and glorious, *as well as* approachable, trustworthy, and loving, will pray with more certainty and faith.

Someone who does not see God in this way may be hindered from praying.

Question 4   Possible answers:

Prayer request	Anticipated heart impact
1. Hope	1. Less anxiety/hopelessness
2. We are his inheritance	2. Deeper security
3. Power	3. Ability to stand, to overcome

Ephesians 3:14–21   Being enabled to receive God's love is the main aim of the second part of Paul's prayer. Lies that distort one's image of God and of self keep people from receiving his love.

Question 6   An example: "May God, who has what it takes, strengthen you in your deepest being."

Question 7   You may want to encourage people to think about the fact that although Christ is in them because they are Christians, he has not yet filled every part of them, or they may not yet have made room for him in every area of their lives.

Question 8   People may realize that they would have the power to surrender such things as the fear of death, of being controlled by money, of an obsession, of a driven life.

Question 12 The Holy Spirit takes an active role in convincing the human heart of biblical truth. Sometimes in order for people to understand and receive God's Father love they need to work through their confusion about human relationships. Someone who has learned that it is dangerous to trust others will also find it hard to trust God. The Holy Spirit helps people to sort out their pain, forgive others, and let go of sinful attitudes and actions rooted in lies. (Some lies can be: "I need to protect myself, so I'll keep my distance from others and God;" "People and God only like me if or when I'm perfect, so I'd better not fail.") We can tell our minds of God's truth, but the Holy Spirit convinces us of it at a heart level.

Responding to God

It is good that people are first specific and honest concerning the lies they have believed, but encourage them to take the further step of seeking the Holy Spirit's help to replace the lies with specific truth.

session three

Reveals the Word
Luke 24:1–32, 45

Purpose: To help group members draw more upon the Holy Spirit's aid when they think about Scripture, especially about the truth of the cross. Luke 24 is an excellent illustration of how people, though they have heard truth many times and even have Jesus with them, do not recognize or connect this truth to their lives.

Engaging the Text

Question 1 Answers may include: It was part of God's plan; it was necessary; Jesus would rise again. People are helped to see that Jesus in fact did all he could to prepare the disciples, but for some reason they were not able to grasp the significance of the cross and how it fit into their lives.

Question 2 Jesus clearly told his disciples all they needed to know to face his death with faith. They have been with him daily and heard him speak on countless occasions. Given all Jesus said and did to prove who he was, it is almost unbelievable that they are confused by the cross and resurrection. Be sure to help people make the connection, however, that when Christians today experience the unexpected in life, they can be thrown into confusion even though they may know Bible verses that could give them perspective. What the disciples needed, and what we need today, is help to work through confusing thoughts and feelings in order to come to deeper certainty and faith.

Question 3 Any of us who struggle with hopelessness, confusion, a sense of abandonment, condemnation, or a defeatist attitude toward sin; or who are slaves to such things as money, sex, ambition, greed, or anger; or who strive to please, to accomplish, or to be good enough, in order to be accepted—live as if the cross never happened. We are then blind to the benefits Jesus offers us today through the Holy Spirit. We are like the two in this story, who need God's help to work through their confusion and come to a deeper understanding of truth.

Question 4 It is possible that God himself is keeping them from seeing him right away so that they are able to process their doubts and fears and come to the place of understanding and faith. It is also possible that their doubts, disillusionment, fear, and unmet expectations are themselves keeping the two from recognizing Jesus. After all, they have had a very specific idea of what the Messiah is going to do for them. They do not want a dead one. They have wanted a Messiah who would free them from Roman rule. This Jesus whom they have been following does not meet those expectations, so he cannot be the one they are looking for.

Question 5 Jesus draws out their feelings and thoughts with questions. He gives them time and space to process their fears. Notice what he does not do. He does not reprimand them for abandoning him at the cross. He has not given up on them but is there walking beside them! He is patient, respectful, interactive. He leads them to the point where they can risk believing the good news that he is in fact alive and with them as he promised. Note the exclamation: "How foolish you are!" In this culture, blunt, emotive conversation is considered normal. Jesus, after listening for quite awhile, is simply making a contribution to their thinking, showing them Scripture that might change their perspective. It still takes hours of conversation before they really get it!

Question 6 He works with us, is patient, asks questions, draws us out, is interested in our feelings and thoughts even if they are confused. He is skilled at leading us to a deeper understanding. It is important to note that it is not appropriate to handle doubt and confusion by simply beating Bible verses into one's head. We need to process thoughts and feelings with God as we consider the truth of Scripture.

Question 10 He opens their understanding of the Scriptures. As they grasp the truth, their perspective, feelings, and direction change.

Question 11 Again, note that true "digestion" of God's Word involves cooperation of our mind and emotions and willingness to receive and/or obey. It is important for people to realize that the Holy Spirit, like Jesus in this story, is working with our hearts to help us digest truth. He does not leave us on our own to get our hearts in order. On the other hand, he does not force us to digest truth but respects us and responds to our invitation to continue his work in us.

session four

Whispers to Us about the Father

Luke 15:11–32; Romans 8:15–16

Purpose: To help people "tune into" or become more sensitive to the voice of the Holy Spirit, who is continuously speaking to the believer about God's Father heart toward each of us. Romans 8:15–16 is the key Scripture passage for the study as it clearly states this truth. The parable in Luke 15:11–32 is complementary to it, giving a picture of the father as well as two different ways to relate to him.

Engaging the Text

Question 2 From the beginning of the story the younger son seems free to approach the father and to make requests of him without feeling the need to first earn this privilege. Even in his destitute state, he is quick to consider approaching his father, although even he thinks he has lost his right as a son. By contrast, the older son seems distant, takes no risks, and is not free to approach his father, even though his father is right there with him.

Question 5 Some suggestions would be:

- Father with younger son: They are interactive with each other; the father respects the son's choice; the son recognizes when he fails the father and takes the responsibility to approach him to ask forgiveness; there is freedom, respect, risk, trust.
- Father with older son: There is very little intimacy; there is very little interaction between them; the relationship appears to be distant.

- Older son with younger son: They do not appear to have any relationship.

Question 9   The Holy Spirit is actively communicating to a believer's spirit, describing God to him or her so that eventually the believer recognizes, *at heart level*, that God is in fact a trustworthy father.

Question 10 Individuals are encouraged to be listening to their hearts, as well as to learn from other people how they receive heart revelation.

Responding to God

Let this time of prayer flow from what has just been discussed in Questions 9 and 10.

session five

Restrains Passion
1 Samuel 25:1–42

Purpose: To help people understand the role of the Holy Spirit in strengthening us to say no to temptation, so that they will cooperate more with him in everyday life. The Holy Spirit's primary strategy in the fight against temptation is to remind believers of who God is and who they as believers are in relation to God. The story of Abigail interacting with David at a crucial moment helps us to see how the Holy Spirit interacts with the believer's conscience.

Engaging the Text

Question 1   David has served Nabal by protecting his property.

Question 2   David shows respect for Nabal. He expects a hospitable response.

Question 3   Nabal slanders David's character, ignores David's voluntary and respectful service, and disregards the custom of generosity at festival time.

Question 4   People are helped to put themselves into David's shoes, feeling the insults and his anger.

Question 5   The group thinks about what it takes to stop and redirect a person who is set on a course of sinful action. Answers may include: David gets perspective that Nabal's insults say more about Nabal than about him; he weighs the consequences of his intended action; he is reminded that his intended action of revenge is below him.

Questions 7 and 8 Abigail uses words that call forth from David the true perspective of the situation as well as the consequences of his present course of action. In a very concrete way, Abigail reminds David that he is more than a person of anger and bloodshed. Some important verses are verse 24, "Let the blame be on me alone," and verse 28, "The LORD will . . . make a lasting dynasty for my master, because he fights the LORD's battles." Abigail wisely reminds David of who he is, which takes the sting out of Nabal's insults.

Question 9 Like Abigail, the Holy Spirit speaks words that reinforce for us the larger and eternal context of our lives. He actively reminds each of us that all sin, even the sin of the one who hurts us most deeply, has been paid for by Jesus. There is no need for any individual to take revenge. The Holy Spirit is also constantly reminding us of our inheritance and destiny in Christ. It is important to encourage group members not just to give a "right" answer here, but to think of examples of how the Holy Spirit has in fact interacted with them. You may want to ask further questions like, "How do you know he is saying that?" The sidebar "The Voice of Righteousness" may also help to illustrate the point.

Hot Topic: You may want to mention that consideration of this question will help people think through the process of sin in real-life circumstances. It is important to recognize that it is possible to say no to sin but that it sometimes takes time. Sometimes specific prayer is needed.

Satisfies Our Heart

John 4:1–27

Purpose: To encourage people to drink from the riches of Christ within them, and to do so through the act of worship. True worship is not essentially an outward matter, but rather what goes on in the heart, inspired by the Holy Spirit. Engaging in true worship satisfies the deepest of human longings.

Engaging the Text

Question 1 The Samaritan woman is most likely recognized by all in the city, but for negative reasons. There is no evidence of family, only that she is sleeping with a man. She appears to be avoiding people by coming to the well at noon when others would not come. There is no evidence that she makes any positive contribution to society.

Question 2 She may be avoiding other women and their criticism, as they would probably detest her for her lifestyle.

Question 4 Jesus has chosen to walk through Samaria even though other Jews thought of Samaritans as "unclean" and a people to avoid. He breaks the cultural barrier by not only talking to a woman but also by asking this "social outcast" to serve him water. He thus treats her with the respect that would be normal for any citizen. Jesus does this because he values every single person, regardless of nationality or deeds.

Question 5 People are helped to realize that this same Jesus approaches them and interacts with them in a similar way. Jesus treats every person with respect and without condemnation. He offers every person the opportunity to serve him, to dialogue with him, regardless of public opinion. He has the power to set each of us free from the sins that entangle us, no matter who we are or what we have done.

Question 6 It is in the heat of the day that a person is likely to be most thankful for fresh, living water to drink. This woman obviously recognizes the value of the gift her forefather has left for her and others. Jesus wants her to tune into her spiritual thirst that no natural water can quench. He offers her himself, the living water, who alone can quench this thirst. This is the best inheritance.

Question 7 People are encouraged to think about the deepest needs of their heart and the reality of the Holy Spirit satisfying their thirst.

Question 8 True worship is not a matter of the right place or form, but of a person's heart responding to the truth of God.

Question 9 True worship activates our heart to receive from the ministry of the Holy Spirit within us.

Question 10 People are encouraged both to *take steps to engage* in more true worship, and to *expect* to drink from the living water within them as they do so.

If you know the Lord, you have already heard his voice—it is that inner leading that brought you to him in the first place. Jesus always checked with his Father (John 8:26–29), and so should we; hearing the voice of the heavenly Father is a basic right of every child of God. The following are a number of ways of fine-tuning this experience:

1 **Hearing God's voice is possible for you!**

Don't make guidance complicated. It's actually hard not to hear God if you really want to please and obey him! If you stay humble, he promises to guide you (Proverbs 16:9). Here are three simple steps to help in hearing his voice:

- *Submit* to his lordship. Ask him to help you silence your own thoughts and desires and the opinions of others that may be filling your mind (2 Corinthians 10:5). Even though you have been given a good mind to use, right now you want to hear the thoughts of the Lord, who has the *best* mind (Proverbs 3:5–6).
- *Resist* the enemy, in case he is trying to deceive you at this moment. Use the authority that Jesus Christ has given you to silence the voice of the enemy (Ephesians 6:10–20; James 4:7).
- *Expect* your loving heavenly Father to speak to you. After asking your question, wait for him to answer. He will (Exodus 33:11; Psalm 69:13; John 10:27).

2 **God speaks in different ways**

Allow God to speak to you in the way he chooses. Don't try to dictate to him concerning the guidance methods you prefer. He is Lord—you are his servant (1 Samuel 3:9). So listen with a yielded heart; there is a direct link between yield-edness and hearing. He may choose to speak to you through *his Word*. This could come in your daily reading of the Bible, or he could guide you to a particular verse (Psalm 119:105). He may speak to you through an *audible voice* (Exodus 3:4), through dreams (Matthew 2), or through *visions* (Isaiah 6:1; Revelation 1:12–17). But probably the most common way is through the quiet *inner voice* (Isaiah 30:21).

3	**Acknowledge your sin before God**	Confess any sin. A clean heart is necessary if you want to hear God (Psalm 66:18).
4	**Revisit the scene of God's guidance**	Use the Axhead Principle (see 2 Kings 6). If you seem to have lost your way, go back to the last time you knew the sharp, cutting edge of God's voice. Then obey. The key question is, "Have you obeyed the last thing God has told you to do?"
5	**God can and will speak to you!**	Get your own leading. God will use others to confirm your guidance, but you should also hear from him directly. It can be dangerous to rely on others to get the word of the Lord for you (1 Kings 13).
6	**God will make it clear in his time**	Don't talk about your guidance until God gives you permission to do so. Sometimes this happens immediately; at other times there is a delay. The main purpose of waiting is to avoid four pitfalls: *pride*—because God has spoken to you; *presumption*—by speaking before you have full understanding; *missing God's timing and method*; and *bringing confusion to others*, who also need prepared hearts (Ecclesiastes 3:7; Mark 5:19; Luke 9:36).
7	**Be alert to the signs God provides**	Use the Wise-Men Principle (see Matthew 2). Just as the wise men individually followed the star and were all led to the same Christ, so God will often use two or more spiritually sensitive people to *confirm* what he is telling you (2 Corinthians 13:1).
8	**Discern true guidance from false guidance**	Beware of counterfeits. Of course you have heard of a counterfeit dollar bill. But have you ever heard of a counterfeit paper bag? No. Why not? Because only things of value are worth counterfeiting. Satan has a counterfeit of everything of God that is possible for him to copy (Exodus 7:22; Acts 8:9–11). Counterfeit guidance comes, for example, through Ouija boards, seances, fortune-telling, and astrology (Leviticus 19:26; 20:6; 2 Kings 21:6). The guidance of the Holy Spirit leads you closer to Jesus and into true freedom. Satan's guidance leads you away from God into bondage. One key test for true guidance: Does your leading follow biblical principles? The Holy Spirit never contradicts the Word of God. Confess any sin. A clean heart is necessary if you want to hear God (Psalm 66:18).

9 | **Yield your heart completely to the Lord** | Opposition from humans is sometimes guidance from God (Acts 21:10–14). The important thing again is yieldedness to the Lord (Daniel 6:6–23; Acts 4:18–21). Rebellion is never of God, but sometimes he asks us to step away from our elders in a way that is not rebellion but part of his plan. Trust that he will show your heart the difference.

10 | **God will reveal your calling** | Every follower of Jesus has a unique ministry (Romans 12; 1 Corinthians 12; Ephesians 4:11–13; 1 Peter 4:10–11). The more you seek to hear God's voice in detail, the more effective you will be in your own calling. Guidance is not a game—it is serious business where we learn *what* God wants us to do and *how* he wants us to do it. The will of God is doing and saying the right thing in the right place, with the right people at the right time and in the right sequence, under the right leadership, using the right method with the right attitude of heart.

11 | **Stay in constant communication with God** | Practice hearing God's voice and it becomes easier. It's like picking up the phone and recognizing the voice of your best friend . . . you know that voice because you have heard it so many times before. Compare the young Samuel with the older man Samuel (1 Samuel 3:4–7; 8:7–10; 12:11–18).

12 | **God wants a relationship with you!** | Relationship is the most important reason for hearing the voice of the Lord. God is not only infinite, but personal. If you don't have communication, you don't have a personal relationship with him. True guidance is getting closer to the Guide. We grow to know the Lord better as he speaks to us; as we listen to him and obey him, we make his heart glad (Exodus 33:11; Matthew 7:24–27).

Loren Cunningham ©1984

PRINCIPLES FOR effective INTERCESSION

1 Praise God for who he is, and for the privilege of engaging in the same wonderful ministry as the Lord Jesus (Hebrews 7:25). Praise God for the privilege of cooperating with him in the affairs of humankind through prayer.

2 Make sure your heart is clean before God by having given the Holy Spirit time to convict, should there be any unconfessed sin (Psalm 66:18; 139:23–24).

3 Acknowledge that you can't really pray without the direction and energy of the Holy Spirit (Romans 8:26). Ask God to utterly control you by his Spirit, receive by faith the reality that he does, and thank him (Ephesians 5:18).

4 Deal aggressively with the enemy. Come against him in the all-powerful name of the Lord Jesus Christ and with the "sword of the Spirit"—the Word of God (Ephesians 6:17; James 4:7).

5 Die to your own imaginations, desires, and burdens for what you feel you should pray about (Proverbs 3:5–6; 28:26; Isaiah 55:8).

6 Praise God now in faith for the remarkable prayer meeting you're going to have. He's a remarkable God, and he will do something consistent with his character.

7 Wait before God in silent expectancy, listening for his direction (Psalm 62:5; 81:11–13; Micah 7:7).

8 In obedience and faith, utter what God brings to your mind, believing (John 10:27). Keep asking God for direction, expecting him to give it to you. He will (Psalm 32:8). Make sure you don't move to the next subject until you've given God time to discharge all he wants to say regarding this burden—especially when praying in a group. Be encouraged by the lives of Moses, Daniel, Paul, and Anna, knowing that God gives revelation to those who make intercession a way of life.

9   If possible, have your Bible with you should God want to give you direction or confirmation from it (Psalm 119:105).

10   When God ceases to bring things to your mind for which to pray, finish by praising and thanking him for what he has done, reminding yourself of Romans 11:36: "For from him and through him and to him are all things. To him be the glory forever! Amen."

A WARNING: God knows the weakness of the human heart toward pride. If we speak of what God has revealed and done in intercession, it may lead to committing this sin. God shares his secrets with those who are able to keep them. There may come a time when he definitely prompts us to share, but unless this happens, we should remain silent: "The disciples kept this to themselves, and told no one at that time what they had seen" (Luke 9:36). "Mary treasured up all these things and pondered them in her heart" (Luke 2:19).

Joy Dawson ©1985

We all have an opportunity to affect the course of history. If we pray with clean hearts, regularly and effectively, for the nations, we become history shapers. We are to pray for all nations and to focus primarily on the body of Christ, the church, as God intends her to shape the course of history. This ministry of intercession also prepares her for future authority in his eternal kingdom (2 Chronicles 7:14; Job 12:23; Psalm 2:8–9; Isaiah 56:7; Daniel 7:27; Revelation 2:26–29).

Here are twelve steps to help you pray more effectively.

1

Thank and praise God for who he is and for:
- The privilege of cooperating with him in prayer.
- His involvement already in the nation for which he is leading you to pray (Philemon 4–6).

2

Pray for an unprecedented outpouring of the Holy Spirit upon the church worldwide (Psalm 85:6; Isaiah 64:1–3):
- That God's people would see that there is no substitute for revival, pray persistently, and be prepared for it. Consider these biblical promises for revival: Psalm 102:15–16; Isaiah 41:17–20; 45:8; 52:10; 59:19; 61:11; Hosea 6:3b; Zechariah 10:1.
- That the church would receive revelation of God's awesome holiness and unfathomable love leading to deep repentance, especially of the sins of idolatry, apathy, and disobedience, resulting in a passionate love for the Lord.

3

Pray for unity in the Body of Christ:
- For revelation of the pride and prejudice that separates.
- That reconciliation would result; success depends on it (Matthew 12:25).
- That seeing their need for each other, they would honor and prefer one another.
- That their manifest unity would influence the lost to come to Jesus Christ (John 17:23).

4   Pray for leaders (Judges 5:2; Psalm 75:7; Proverbs 8:13–15; 29:18; Ephesians 4:11):
- For spiritual leaders to be raised up who understand the character and ways of God and fear him.
- To receive vision related to the extension of God's kingdom worldwide.
- For righteous leaders to be placed into all spheres of authority and influence (Proverbs 28:2).
- That God would convict unrighteous leaders, and if they persist in sin, overthrow them.

5   Pray that God's Word would have its rightful place:
- As the basis for laws, moral values, and behavior (Psalm 119:126).
- That preachers and teachers would get their messages from God's Word, and live them and teach them (Jeremiah 23:22; 1 Corinthians 4:16–17).

6   Pray that God's people would see that obedience is the key to the Christian life, that God's priorities would become theirs (Psalm 19:11–14; 34:1; Proverbs 8:13; Matthew 4:10, 19; 2 Corinthians 7:1):

- A life of worship, praise, and intercession.
- Time alone with God, getting to know him through his Word, and waiting on him for directions.
- Having a heart burdened for the lost and witnessing to them.
- A biblical understanding and practice of the fear of the Lord that would permeate every believer's life.
- Fulfilling the conditions to be empowered by the Holy Spirit (Ephesians 5:18).

7   Pray for children and youth:
- To have the chance to be born, hear the gospel, and know that God loves them—that deliverance and healing would come to the abused and neglected.
- That God would raise up anointed ministries to teach them the character and ways of God.
- For revival to come among them.

8 Pray for workers:
- To be sent to every nation and from every nation (Matthew 9:38; 28:19–20).
- That every believer would embrace the mandate "Go to the nations," and seek the necessary grace to stay home if God so directs.

9 Pray for an increased effectiveness of the varied media ministries targeted to reach the lost.

10 Engage in spiritual warfare (Matthew 16:18):
- Against satanic attacks on both the church and the unsaved.
- Ask God to reveal principalities dominating nations and cities. Pray against them (Ephesians 6:12–13; James 4:7; Revelation 12:11).

11 Pray for spiritual awakening of the unconverted, motivating them to seek God:
- Salvation of unrighteous leaders.
- Radical conversions of most unlikely people, resulting in powerful ministries.
- Revelation to come to the ignorant and the deceived of Jesus' deity and claims, with resultant conversions.

12 Release faith:
- That your prayers are being answered (John 14:13; 16:24; 2 Peter 3:9)!
- That the nations will fear him. Praise God that he will rebuild his church and appear in his glory (Psalm 102:15–16).

Joy Dawson ©1990

WORLD Map

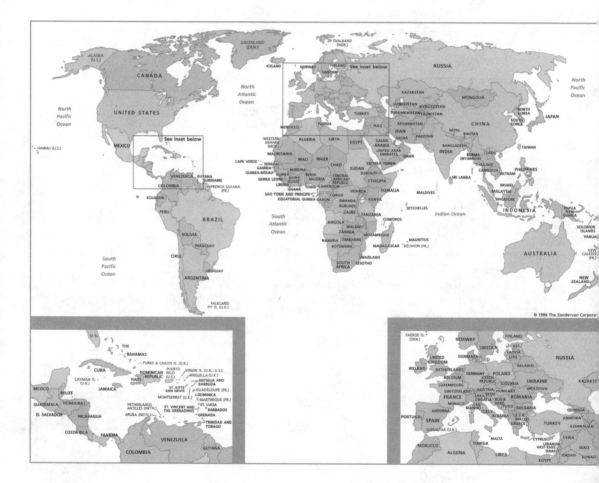

© 1996 The Zondervan Corporation

stay CONNECTED!

Living Encounters Series
Youth With A Mission

Styled after Youth With A Mission's (YWAM) successful Discipleship Training School (DTS), the Living Encounters series draws on YWAM's years of experience and expertise in training people of all ages for international ministry. Its unique, life-changing approach to Bible study will expand your small group's paradigm of Christianity . . . liberate its spiritual passion . . . and fill it with the joy and spiritual vigor that come from following an unpredictable, radical, and totally amazing risen Lord.

Experiencing the Spirit: *Living in the Active Presence of God*   0-310-22706-2
Seeing Jesus: *The Father Made Visible*   0-310-22707-0
Encountering God: *The God You've Always Wanted to Know*   0-310-22708-9
Building Relationships: *Connections for Life*   0-310-22709-7
Embracing God's Grace: *Strength to Face Life's Challenges*   0-310-22229-X
Expanding Your View: *Seeing the World God's Way*   0-310-22704-6
Making God Known: *Offering the Gift of Life*   0-310-22703-8
Finding Your Purpose: *Becoming All You Were Meant to Be*   0-310-22702-X

Look for Living Encounters at your local Christian bookstore.
ZondervanPublishingHouse

About Youth With a Mission

The Heart of Youth With A Mission

Youth With A Mission (YWAM) is an international movement of Christians from many denominations dedicated to presenting Jesus Christ personally to this generation, to mobilizing as many as possible to help in this task, and to training and equipping believers for their part in fulfilling the Great Commission. As Christians of God's Kingdom, we are called to love, worship, and obey our Lord, to love and serve his body, the Church, and to present the whole gospel for the whole man throughout the whole world.

We in Youth With A Mission believe that the Bible is God's inspired and authoritative Word, revealing that Jesus Christ is God's Son; that man is created in God's image; and that he created us to have eternal life through Jesus Christ; that although all men have sinned and come short of God's glory, God has made salvation possible through the death on the cross and resurrection of Jesus Christ.

We believe that repentance, faith, love, and obedience are fitting responses to God's initiative of grace toward us; that God desires all men to be saved and to come to the knowledge of truth; and that the Holy Spirit's power is demonstrated in and through us for the accomplishing of Christ's last commandment: "Go into all the world and preach the good news to all creation" (Mark 16:15).

Evangelism — spreading God's message.
Training — preparing workers to reach others.
Mercy Ministries — showing God's love through practical assistance.

Youth With A Mission has a particular mandate for mobilizing and championing the ministry potential of young people. But our worldwide missions force also includes thousands of older people from all kinds of social, cultural, ethnic, and professional backgrounds. Our staff of 12,000 includes people from more than 135 nations and ranges from relatively new Christians to veteran pastors and missionaries.

We are committed to a lifestyle of dependence on God for guidance, financial provision, and holy living. We also affirm a lifestyle of worship, prayer, godly character, hospitality, generosity, servant leadership, team ministry, personal responsibility, and right relationships with one another and our families.

Because of its visionary calling, YWAM does new things in new ways where new initiatives are required. We seek to build bridges among Christian leaders, partnering with local churches and missions for completion of the Great Commission. Annually, over 35,000 people from various churches take part in YWAM's short-term outreach projects.

Teams from Youth With A Mission have now ministered in every country of the world and have ministry centers in 142 nations, but the work is far from complete. We welcome all who want to know God and make him known to join with us in finishing the task — to "make disciples of all nations" (Matthew 28:19).

for more information

For more information about YWAM, please contact YWAM Publishing to obtain YWAM's *Go Manual*, an annual directory of YWAM's addresses and training and service opportunities (send $5 to cover costs), or write one of our field offices for more information. Note: Please mention the Living Encounters Bible study series in your request for information.

YWAM Field Offices

Youth With A Mission
(The Americas Office)
P.O. Box 4600
Tyler, TX 75712 U.S.A.
1–903–882–5591

Youth With A Mission
(Europe, Middle East, & Africa Office)
Highfield Oval, Harpenden
Herts. AL5 4BX
England, U.K.
(44) 1582–463–300

Youth With A Mission
(Pacific & Asia Office)
P.O. Box 7
Mitchell, A.C.T. 2911
Australia
(61) 6–241–5500

YWAM International DTS
(Discipleship Training School) Centre
PF 608
Budapest 62
1399 Hungary
100726.1773@compuserve.com

YWAM Publishing

P.O. Box 55787
Seattle, WA 98155 U.S.A.
Phone: 1–800–922–2143 (U.S. only) or
1–425–771–1153
Fax: 1–425–775–2383
E-mail address:
75701.2772@compuserve.com
Web page:
www.ywampublishing.com

DISCOVER YOUR PERSONAL PATH
TOWARD INTIMACY WITH GOD

CHRISTIAN GROWTH STUDY BIBLE
New International Version

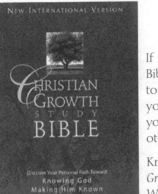

If you've enjoyed this YWAM study guide, you'll love this YWAM study Bible! The *Christian Growth Study Bible* is designed to help you cultivate heart-to-heart closeness with God. The kind you've longed for and God created you for. A dynamic, growing relationship so vital and life-changing that you can't keep it to yourself—you've got to tell the world about it and help others discover the greatness of your heavenly Father.

Knowing God and Making Him Known is the heartbeat of the *Christian Growth Study Bible*. It's also the heartbeat of Youth With A Mission (YWAM). Which is why this Bible's study program is modeled after YWAM's proven approach in their Discipleship Training Schools. At last, here's a study Bible with a 30-path program that will help you take the uncertainty out of your Christian growth. It helps you determine where you are on the path toward maturity—and helps remove the guesswork about where to go from there.

This *Christian Growth Study Bible* will be an invaluable tool for you to use with your Living Encounters Bible study series, giving you further help on the topics you will be exploring.

Hardcover   ISBN 0-310-91809X
ISBN 0-310-918138 Indexed

Softcover   ISBN 0-310-918103

Black Bonded Leather   ISBN 0-310-91812X
ISBN 0-310-918154 Indexed

Burgundy Bonded Leather   ISBN 0-310-918111
ISBN 0-310-918146 Indexed

We want to hear from you. Please send your comments about this
book to us in care of the address below. Thank you.

ZondervanPublishingHouse
Grand Rapids, Michigan 49530
http://www.zondervan.com